Confluences

To Larry
in friendship

Confluences

Allan Briesmaster (signature)

Allan Briesmaster

April 23, 2011
at Mayberry Art Gallery

Seraphim Editions

Cover Design and Typography: Julie McNeill, McNeill Design Arts
Cover Artwork and Author Photo: Holly Briesmaster

Library and Archives Canada Cataloguing in Publication

Briesmaster, Allan
Confluences / Allan Briesmaster.

Poems.
ISBN 978-0-9808879-6-9

I. Title.

PS8553.459C65 2009   C811'.54   C2009-905110-9

Published by
Seraphim Editions
54 Bay St.
Woodstock, ON N4S 3K9
www.seraphimeditions.com

Printed and bound in Canada

For My Friends

Contents

IV. The Vaster Stream

I. Antiquity

By Ancient Starlight

The stars are shy over the parapet,
and I of them – much as
I aspire to friendship.

But no matter how clear
they ever shine,
my eyes lack scope or scale.

I keep craning, though.
And sometimes your stride

comes closer in, Orion, and
you, Corona Borealis, float
much lovelier, shimmering on
the spherical stream, than shapes
the blank daylight provides.

In thanks I configure for you,
and for some like me, these few
long-scattered and dotted burns
of the black light of words.

Antiquity

Across the distance into the ancient time,
up from the layered tills and the rubble-mounds,
flow traces less than the smoke from extinct hearths
around the stubs of pillars, from staked-out pits
in excavations, through museum cases,
on, among the projects of the living hand.

Labels bestowed on the fragments, notions parsed,
interpolated, spliced, decipher some ways
the avatars, at zenith, plausibly walked
and bonded, kept house, warred, and thought and believed.

Unburnt scrolls, in their devoutly copied fractions,
the bits of shattered tablets, glyphs on half-walls
bewilder with their loose disintegration.
But more than the lopped statues and the defaced
bas-reliefs, the pot-shards, amphoras, and all
the amulets, oil lamps, vials, coins, there are words
whose lips can re-open the long tombs of dust.

Imagination and empiricism,
together listening with their unlike ears,
audit the irretrievable. Fancies, facts,
conjectures, and frail scrapings sift into life
when diligent obsession and adept care
incline the patient pupil to be convinced
they were as ignorant and cruel as we are,
hospitable and charged with naked courage,
fierce, awe-stricken, and noble beyond our reach.

In suffering, in impassiveness toward pain
they dwarf us. And in natural genius:
adjacent to the origins of all things.

✧ ✧ ✧

What sages they had when the wide world was fresh!
First law-givers. Before them, the myth-makers.

The rooftops fell. Even the thickest of walls
succumbed to time's and barbarism's rough thrusts.
As offspring of the Vandals and Visigoths,
we linger in the ruins of their ruins,
incompetent to own their virtuous powers,
though sharing flaws that opened the ways to here.

Their scripts fared better, mostly, than did their stone.
Their words continue under-layering ours.
Our twilight still comes tinted with their breath.

Fire Spirit

So we must imagine, and not
    deduce, the dim past.
Let loose the flame that creates,
    unlike what leaves ash.

Bright-hot mental blade – struck across
    the flints of what was.
Ligature for leaping tongues:
    from what was, unto is.

Clairvoyant faith, positing
    an inflammable arc,

the fiercest credence burns on
    through the rinds of the dark.

Temple of Fire

a threshold

In primeval time, the forests' quiet breadth,
enrobed in towering gloom, must have been fearsome:
hunting-ground for terrors on the prowl
by night, canopy of filtered awe throughout
the cautious trails blazed inward from broad day.

What kept the beasts of night back but our fires?
What fended off the unknown, or half-tamed it,
but flames from tongues of words? Both light-givers
became tough tool and a manipulable risk;
forge-heater, and brand; hearth-warmer, transformer …

Then straighter arrow, sharper spear brought boldness.
The finer the axeblade, the clearer grew
the round of safety and simple wealth. The last
wild edgeless animated spirits, high and low,
retreated up the peaks, then took to air.

Trees were for masts. For lumber. Planks, beams.
Or merely felled to fields or empty waste.
Meanwhile the spirits had condensed into
the lofty pantheon who dwelt and roamed far off
from lessening woods, in deep sky and the sea.

How could they be invoked again except
by worship in a worthily sacral space:
a chamber from which heard, effectual pleas
and praise could rise. What roof-supports, what kinds of sides
were fittest for arcaded symmetries

but carven columned stone, to simulate
perfection – dim paths of memory
stemmed-from and rooted back onto the foremost
cross-threshold gasp at pillared groves … configuring
direct, as-yet-unviolated spirit.

Then there would be installed the priest, not shaman,
with tenders of the tame symbolic spark
beside an altar.
                    But fire, thrown by lightning,
had been the unknown spur of woodland cycles;
and human fire, as much, leaves only ash.

                    ✧ ✧ ✧

Our air is a slow fire, as is the sunlight,
and careless flames explode, and singe, and char.
And yet our minds view both the actual fire
and the imagined as a fountainhead of change.
It rids us of dead matter, it refines

what's less destructible. We seek for it,
and feel the absence as a poverty.
It defies the cold stillness in what's dark,
supplants the limits given us within the sun.
Images our faint knowledge of the stars.

But no tribe had a temple to fire alone –
despite these many magic properties –
while granting that the sun does not suffice.
A fiery temple may be wrought of words, though, if
a mind's own sun kindles the natal flame.

Yet, after the inflammable stuffs burn off,
the paths fires clear, in time, are also gone.
Because we mortals flame our lives away,
our earthly life itself, for us, is fearful change.
So even the literal temples become kindling

for rebirth of successor groves of stone,
or, one fine day, a groundwork to a forest,
out of the wildfire that unlocks the cone –
though we resist the planar notion of a circle,
and wish our flames to lick some wilder zone ...

In One of the Dry Places

We hush, the land and I,
awaiting some drastic turn –
the first thunderclap,
first crack on the pillar,
the creak in the stanchion of things.

A sky taut with dryness
denudes the hillsides,
crumbles the soil
and invites winding dunes.
It means to level.

Furious wind feels imminent,
with a billowing prelude –
but nothing lies less
desolately loose
than my own detached glare.

Exiled land, lapsing or gone
to gravel, grit and dust – were there
ever vines to deter us? Wet
roots, one time, dug down deep
against the sift of the ground?

A Sketch of a Kouros

I.

Statuette – cut *into* stone, more than out of stone –
of a youth who steps with an air midway between
unformed boy and the effigy of Apollo.
Archaism concretized. Surface pounded with chisels
opaquing and prepping it for the pigments long-lost.

Neither chthonically crude nor pleasingly smoothened
in your squarish muscles and arms nearly fused to your hips.
Once figure of power. Approximate, stiff. Slightly smiling
and yet transcendental expression which almost escapes
formulaic geometry crossed with a stony restraint.

Half Greek, half Egyptian. A fresh breakthrough in
the evolved medium, *and* inferior echo. Offered
to decorate a temple, perhaps, by somebody
important, or memento of a friend deceased.
Not any person, though. God, warrior, athlete …

No, this came before portraiture; and is not distant
from totemic magic. Devotional marker, created
for touch, for high placement, as focus for simple belief.
Without torsion or the motion of story. Plain symbol:
the evocator of Idea. Endless youth, free of age.

II.

What different potency, statuette, you emit now,
in your cooled, penumbral, glass-protected estate,
millennia since the flickerings of your slow birth
and since you were smashed and burnt by the Persian horde,
then given mass burial on the Acropolis.

Hovering, very few generations ahead
of rough wooden stylized symbol with intimate use,
en route toward perfected public image, on view
as prestigious Art much more than as purposeful thing.
(Though already you bear the patron's or artist's name.)

Still far from figures bodying the Golden Time,
admired for themselves alone, without leadings-beyond,
no longer serving as humble iconic signpost –
how irresistibly you prompt the pre-guided gaze
toward pale eclipsing splendours you clearly fore-ran.

Is it conceivable that any advancement out
of our own immature, lavish barbarousness
could reveal us to those poking our obsolete ruins –
we, who misplace the sacred and embrace our decay –
somehow as "archaic" precursors of finer ways?

Archaic Woman

The strict form of the temple won't contain you,
nor the agora wholly shut you out.
The dealers in the words and coins and goods there still
transport you, through the temples of moved thought,
across familial into nameless bounds.

Unthanked, you bore their rising civilization,
nurturing it, without what we call love
from those who looked on passion as dementia,
by the long bond to child, and child of child,
with tight commitment keeping the entire house.

If dowry, quiet tact, fertility,
grace, the whole dark, impassive "feminine,"
were stable, though, what made us what we became?
Only wars and inventions? Invasions, migrations?
You laid your own strong, tender templates down

before The Individual broke into being
from noble and tyrant; while assorted gods,
gross monsters and grandiose heroes muscled the core
of stories and their slight off-centre females
remained curved mirrors for manly desire and dread.

A patience beyond articulate conception,
more deeply absorbed in Demeter than Atalanta,
held fiery ova of hope, and you brooded on them
with tight commitment, taking the entire house
across the familial into the nameless grounds.

At Heraclitean War

It should be understood that war is the common condition,
that strife is justice, and that all things come to pass
through the compulsion of strife. – Heraclitus

But if you mean by "war" *unending struggle,*
hot opposition, rough contention – then
I'm in agreement, ancient sage of flame.

The wedge and ploughshare that impels and drives
the dialectic through our restless lives
wrings constant combat: over scarcities,
for which deep urges and desires make claim,
when these can not be portioned or shared out;
and any rule or dictum pits resistance,
arouses and invokes some turnabout.

Every assertion conjures its negation.
We lay waste, clearing paths for newer birth.
Flame's petals yield the seedlings of creation:
hard dragon's teeth sown in volcanic Earth.

Pythagoras Underground

after a drawing by H.B.

Geometer of music's harmony:
the even intervals one plucks
along a vibrant string;

imperious measurement, with exact tune
accompanying, temperately
above uncouth passion

like serene planetary spheres aglide,
while, at the centre, the calm sage
or demigod courts thought.

Only – the earth demurs;
it quakes, dislodges pillars from
square housings in their golden rectangles

to crack on infirm rock
spasmed with random aftershock:
just as some theorems waver and break,

thrust by dire happenstance
or deep contrary rift along
what was once deemed a stolid underpinning.

✧ ✧ ✧

So here he sits, below-ground, the grand mind
without disciples now, bereft
of circling symmetry,

darkened and wearing his right triangle
as if it brained him, in the guise
of dunce cap: while, on top,

lie disjunct ruins lit with crackling fires
that spilled from hearth and brazier and
ran uncontrollably.

Now will simple remorse
inhibit further songs of thought,
apart from sullen rumbles or laments,

or will he reconstruct
a less secure cosmology
as act of intellectual penitence?

Does this defeated vault
echo skeletal consolation –
knowledge that 3 and 4 and 5 stand firm?

Water Sages

(Thales and Anaximander)

And if the source of all is not in myth,
will it be found and grasped somehow by thought?

The gods, no longer operant on things,
become nonsensical to luminous minds
which discern natural laws, make measurements,
are able to forecast the sun's eclipses,
and fix the solstices within their year.

Then, has whatever now exists proceeded
from one *material*, infused everywhere,
or from some imperceptible principle?

Is the prime universal substance Water,
that feeds and floats this round earth from below;
or is there, behind it, and air and fire,
a limitless constituent, out of whose flow
things separate, and back to which they'll go?

And if that source remains beyond thought's reaches,
in all the discourses and theories since
those two Milesian sages' first exchanges –

might mythic dark still yield a deeper glimpse?

Hestia Exposed

Apollo and Poseidon wanted you
as bride. So, to keep peace within Olympus,
you vowed perpetual virginity
and veiled yourself beside the sacred hearth,
tending – embodying – its life of flame.

Yours is the shy vitality without which
home can afford no safety and no nurture.
Gentle and modest, patient and attentive.
Should some fool ever ask, "What does she *do*,"
the best retort would simply be, "She *is*."

Está – maintainer of earthen foundations,
grounding the household in the glowing fire
that lets all dwell together without fear,
keeps children snug inside home's inner walls,
cooks favourite food, and lights the ample table.

The old Greeks, with their outdoor public art,
made her few temples and few images,
and fewer tales – though sometimes they invoked her,
placing her central in a pantheon
preponderantly volatile and fickle.

✧ ✧ ✧

I think you could be wisest of all, Hestia.
My sole imaginary dread for you
(although this should be plain impossible)
is that you might one day be caught outside
unsheltered, without shawl or woven flame

to wrap you: in a time when homes are shattered,
when primal sense of centre and of floor
lapses until the memory of what "hearth"
and hospitable household meant has flown.
But then wouldn't we cease to have been human?

At that point you might need to marry Ocean
or be the mistress of the imperial Sun,
and take dolphins or eagles as familiars,
if any are left after the reign of men.
Or deities outlast the bond with them.

II. Impress of Waters

To the April Rain
for L. S.

Is anything so thin as April rain –
this hush of glided mist, that washes green;
our awakener into an alternate dream,

bearer of soft pangs of restlessness,
far-distance healer, whose cool humid gauze
instills fresh height along a wounded ground.

You sprinkler through the deep-sky-shaded scilla,
smoothener of tracks pressed in harsh dust
where swollen necessary sunlight hurts us numbly,

dries too quickly by its rolling blare,
and renders objects "objects," plain and clear,
with sides, points, grooves emplaced, that swim loose now.

Don't let straight rays divert us from your flow:
tomorrow's warm bewilderment toward summer,
later today, the slant under the dark.

Now by moist breaths too slight for any drenching
spread your indefinite twilight past old marks.
Blend the strange null with the familiar Almost.

Transport – hold – where our eyes forgot we are.

Sightings of the Mountains

(in the Rockies, Jasper to Banff)

Abode of great flowings-away.
Bare source for a soundless
calling some hear:
to dare extend our dimensions.

From topmost peaks, which hold
the first and last pink blushes of days.
Whose cloven shade and tall cold
still harbour the glaciers.

Who raise layer-caking stripes
of a year-round snow,
then lower, through May,
the declivity-filling ermine ribbons.

Founts for the cataracts feeding
the loud savage streams and ultimate plains.
The midway fastnesses, dropping walls
that weep and stain tall waterfalls.

Faceted sides with vertiginous grooves
where avalanches and
unstoppable slides have fanned
on down into thick-rubbled bases of scree.

Grey-brown mansions with rough tilted lawns
of cloudy forests.
The moist nurseries
for turquoise lakes, way-below, which feed

the valley-deepening flume
with its plunge and quiver
in whitewater roar, then lapse
onto silted coils of meandering river.

Masses enmassed, whose outlines jut
the rock-and-white summits that seem grown
immune to temporality
but for that of the sun.

Stern shapes that mount, unwordingly,
up, out of the gape of mind
like the mad impulse toward becoming
irresistibly stringent and wild:

spurning gravity by dint of pure
ascent with sheer physical might;
of supremacy, of prevalence over
all else in weight and in height

which nothing but eternity subdues.
Where none or few
gain momentary purchase and don't die,
while some, adjacent, might more finely live.

Past what an unaided eye
can hope to light on or ever imbue.
Long waves of frozen motion, bearing through:
far beyond earthly cry.

May 2008

Urban Pastoral with Crows

mid-Toronto

A small dank stream keeps a soiled ravine
tree-cloaked below glass-hard glares
off multiplying towers.
It harbours blossom, frond and seed
along an unshapen swath of tints
and tattery shade.

Often from my own tower, over
a wide, deepgreen lake of maples,
I briefly wing the bird in the eye
along the wind where the branch-clouds go
through uncut light, or hang as
feather-snow, and a day or an hour
quieten the expanse.

At times through mid Spring, paired finches
loose vivid trills on the balcony rail.
One otherwise ordinary noon, no
gull wheeled; a falcon was diving.
Mild mornings, if I'm early, crows –
two flicks of black – seize bare limb-tips
at shouting-distance, trading laughs.

Then, in a black-burnt voice of their own,
crows that have roosted and scavenged in me
caw back, and back, and away.

Two Snails

1. On a Bright Leaf

By gray
loops of dung:
the lacqued spiral
takes time. Clung
prisms blister
in slime.

2. Ascending

Eye-horns, up
weed-limb
… lead-climb;

with what
stately pace,
rise: one
foot
on slime!

An Impress of Waters

Mostly it returns full-bodily and
full-spiritedly, when a broad wet wind
smacks bullets of rain at my brow, and buffets
the whole of me, pressing on-into me, all
brute-brusque and utterly cool – and I go
back to Kodiak. Rushing streams, black-sand shore.

And before very long comes the sun of those days
made mainly from wind and rain.
And the North Pacific nears, opening endlessly.

✧ ✧ ✧

Deepgreen of tall, lush grasses and bushes
climbing the creases and limbs on the small mountains
(Pillar, and Pyramid, and Barometer)
soaked its cool-glowing stain in, and later
flushed those wide shoulders with faint-fuchsia swaths
of fireweed. Then the late-summer streams
ran silver-red with the big salmon, whose
million curved backs were writhing shoals you could
walk right across.

Soon, from that, a lone,
finned moment splits out: the one special one, scented
wetgreen and darkly aglow in the shine
of lowering sun on a swift-running creek
near the sea. The always islanding sea.

✧ ✧ ✧

… That one stream you stood in, inside your hipwaders,
that rushed up-against your thighs – where you cast
(not expecting a catch) your line tipped with its
red-and-white spinning Daredevil.

It was not
the tug of fish-muscle there, that those thighs
held forever-imprinted, down vessel and cell,
but that from the meeting waters – fresh
with salt – in the sinuous thrust by the current
and telltale nudge of the turning tide
from its pull by a not-so-distant
untrodden moon.

✧ ✧ ✧

Now what else can be
understood in this more-than-lunarly distanced
prime after-time, lodged-behind an insatiate,
unrelenting mainland road?
Out here:
baneful drizzled domain
of the urbane-mundane. And what in it,
in me, still strides, rears, remains
two-pillared, un-ruined, subsistent in thews
and sinews that run on through the letting-
go of those still-standing limbs?
The wind
and the fresh wild rain left to me, muscling
unlost light across earth and sea.

Autumn

Half-tilted, again broken bright-in-gloom,
glide the unbearable
unveilings of the Beautiful
in full withdrawal: thin
and thinning shine among tree brows,
past misty scarves on lower limbs of light,
and nightly rime in the red glade's dark nooks
behind an empty pond that spreads its own
still introspections – wrinkling off, when wind
picks up and strips another layer

until dull rain completes the laying bare.

Green Music

More potent than grey noise from street and from sky,
and than my cortical buzz, Green Music, in-flows
your tremolo as you shake through the tall, full leaves
this darkening fragrant wind has been playing upon:
sprung up from the level light that now draws out and spurs
the farewell cries from gathered last beaks of the day.

Green Music! arisen again just before the warm dawn:
along the faint dawn-breath stirred by the breaking-forth light,
and at swell and soar of the next unredding sun,
with choral welcome from fresh birds of this newborn day
you blossom so goldenly throughout all instruments
of the whole airy, melodious wakening round ...

Now must a restless, doubt-filling mind intervene?

The sunset's green music had tragic pathos enwound
within its inexorable, slight bittersweet chill.
And the dawn brought something pre-human in: swifter still
(the reverse of lingering) with an onrush more cruel
through the press and pierce of its one fine thoughtless chord,
which silences dreams. Which summons up toil, toll, and tool.

(Then the taunt of the green tone withdraws
one more night, one more day.)

Autumn Came

on time, bearing
the classic, quiet fiery
messages. The clear
code in the ripening trees
and all.

Yesterday I read
on her unprinted gown
of sky (the one
with the goldenrod-and-aster hem)
the welcoming

it would have been inhuman to refuse.
And touched, like Braille,
the embossed volume
she proffered, holding the works
of life and death.

✧ ✧ ✧

Back in the full of June, when green-
violet seedheads on the meadow
first embrowned, I had
anticipated, but
language and melody

were missing. Melancholy mixed
with delicious longing gave
plenty to preoccupy
the illiterate heart.
Rainbows would bend

sometimes, after the thunderstorms,
and I adored the way
the cordilleras of the cumulus,
on turning mellowgold,
increased the air,

then drew apart
in solemn coral-pink tone
to a stupendous coast.
And later, savoured
the upsprung sundown wind.

✧ ✧ ✧

Those days, believing I
loved best the world this one
only shadowed and now and
then tantalizingly
fore-ran,

     I plain ignored
     the singe-off of
     nebulous blossom,
     and left unnoted, after the slate-
     and-ash collapse, above,

how the night city painted
a shroud of steam.
Noon after noon saw dimly my
denial of the lunar
dark. Of solar dark.

        ❖ ❖ ❖

     Now in this gifted season,
     when mortal music's tremolo
     swells field and glade, and the inequity
     of night compounds,
     the debt

comes legible that I
must pay earth, the maternal sky
and patient friends: without
back-interest of the least
cosmic regret.

Strata Before Sunset

The cream colour the evening clouds take on,
　　up-spread puffed filaments, at cordial stretch.

　　Prismatic moistly rose-pearled oval patch,
transluced a distance off the invisible sun.

A strip, cleared applegreen along one rift-way;
　　topmost ribbed raft, last flotsam, clung sheer-white.

A low shoal that revalues, now it's gone grey,
　　all-snow and coloured coasts' high lingered light.

Then comes the inevitable contrail with a jet's
　　plumbed thunder, thrust below ground-traffic's flight.

Still, tuned so toward cloud-rhythm, heart forgets
　　the qualities of any lower air:

　　suspended, skied, gaped in a passive stare
wild for a taintless beauty tapering there.

Dec. 31 '08

Noon of clear sun on new snow,
through icicles, along ledges, into
these evergreen shrubbery boughs
over lavender shadow –

Day for the inner eye, home,
fed, comforted out the window by
grey-white juncos, puffed with down,
that hop beside the trellis, pick seeds –

This afternoon quiet, fulfilling even
as the slow slope of the light
(the brief birds gone) starts to slide the mind
apart from the wing –

                ✧ ✧ ✧

So I go out to taste the bright cold. – Severe!
All fresh. Restored from late height.

Not exhaust, not fear; a sense of repair
for once is breathing across today's air.

Will Hope be the "new norm" next year?

III. Conditions

Call

Stellar divination,
sheddings of fire and air,
    You
        vertiginous
lucid rapture
    fallen from over
        the filling moon,

take me toward words
    with precise teeth,
enraged, to rend
    the blank, dull, numb –
        every such drawn
barrier.

      – Until
   and until
      the long-brokenness
itself   break, and be
  broken through.

Reflections on *Gojou*

"the Five Passions"

1.

So much that's human, to rage at. – Fat gut of a self-
stupefying self-satisfaction: such that
it would insult pigs to compare. Then the fraudulent ones,
who cart off their bacon. Oiled with it. Hate them, hate them
incomparably to maligned wolves and the pretty weasels.

2.

How little joy, ever. Sporadic! Yet how far the ripples.
The child's large glee, absorbed yet conscious in flow
amid earliest feats. Then, moments, possibly,
of the honeymoon: threshold on sweet ocean.
Then beach crossed again in the steps of one's own small child.

3.

Wouldn't it be best to detach ourselves from desire?
From wanting what's way beyond reach, what's destined to slip
our grasp and retention and fly and fade past recall.
But what other force can spur us on toward the rare joys?
Though what else will pave the inevitable trail of grief?

4.

There's that phase in your grieving when an anger grips.
It crushes you for your failure not to foresee
and prevent this loss, intervene; not have given more care
to the living one. Blind anger, too, at those others
who just don't get it. And then, at the lost one himself.

5.

Hatred. It's not a vacating of love, as they say.
Could also be well-justified. Or be a mutation
from caring for someone deeply desired, who strays,
who betrays. And, it's well to hate what's plain wrong, only not
the wrongdoer. *If* no hatefulness coils in you too.

Passions, Revisited

Hate What
Self-satisfied stupidity irks worst.
My fist pounds futilely on its deaf wall.
Then hypocritical prevarications.
Then puffs of baseless yet superior airs
pass casual, vacant acid on kind skins.

Vanishing Joy
Can feelings and the words once used for them –
like "mirth," "good cheer," and "joy" and "gaiety" –
breathe past the numb fume of our sophistry,
connote, and signify, without some sneer
that scorches even the pink lungs of the child?

Desire's Rewards
What drives the world besides desire for more?
This muscle. Engine of our lengthening stretch …
Gain, and prevail, and grasp – still never enough.
(Beyond intelligence, the wishful soar.)
So scant the pith of taste, so slick the touch.

Grief, Part 2
For those most widely stricken with this wound,
no closure comes until we're through death's doors.
Let others gauze a sill of resolution –
and I'll admit I'm growing caulked by scars –
but the main cut still rives the floor and ground.

A Use for Anger
I realize I'll never turn serene
in ways the godlier and wise ones own.
What good I do gets fired and fueled by rage:
my slant revenge on those who once demeaned,
returning work of worth beyond demand.

Worse

What can be left wild and whole,
escaping the rabid mutations
that chase us out of our souls?

The core wants its ground to forebear,
but procurement of brass horizons
desecrates anything near.

(Behind all, the "i" without "you."
Without we. The we without i.
The reactive acid, the stiff passive glue.)

Toxic hate and coldwired, brute
rampaging grasp, crush and slash –
wristed by cunning. More grave, more acute …

So the fearfully timid lie bowed
too lazy for thought or long looks.
Couched in immobile dread; cowed

while the thick efflux deepens its piles,
the ponds cloud and film. While the air,
spewed-through with soot, turns vile.

But what stinks worse now than despair
is the staying snugly unaware,
and a vacant refusal to care.

Lines for the Slumberized

Will children, after this
clouded cupidity
and its relentless fire,
see any green repair?
Not if you, I, and ours
sleep on, inert in the
comfort of a despair
no more effectual than
a misdirected prayer.

March 10, 2007

The Inuit report that the sun this year
has broken above their winter night horizons
in February, not April – apparently due
to altered thickness of the southern air.

Experts have just discovered how the soot
from China soars far over the Pacific
to heighten the jet-stream-diverting storms
that splintered the old groves in Stanley Park.

Tonight America moves daylight up
some three weeks earlier than ever before.
A timely power-cutting measure, when
the worldwide fuel reserves run somewhat low.

I feel as if the tipping point is passed now,
so gross the burnup. Excess effluents
have spewed too long and too deep to retract.
Still, better a pained conscience than a sleeper's.

Having already lost two hours of sleep,
I waken reluctantly for further nightmare.
At least I write by a fluorescent bulb –
taking a small belated measure or two.

So even if it's too late to unclock the worst,
I'll turn the gas down under the nearest flame.

Atmosphere, October 2008

Feared fire, and fired fear, and spook and smoke
with ingrained, thickening smudges on the air
repulse old schoolroom notions of horizon,
stifle all breaths except what raises hair.

Tall cranes beyond the flickered penthouse windows
deafen to their foreclosing destinies;
lack second guess, lack hedge. Can't calm but stir
the terror. Silver fled out of the mirror.

The broken news tolls only the gross break-ins.
Not enough wind-blades to cool coal's black front.
Through plasma, indefinite warfares gurgle
sound-bytes dispensed by wounds of want and won't.

On Twisted Streets

after Pierre Reverdy, "Chemin Tournant"

Calamitous brown smog presses in

Windless inverted smoke from forests and the sulphured coal

Traffic swishes through a stealthy dusk

And in the sweat-wet night mouths whine and groan

Corroded metals line the bank of tongue

Pounding bass-acrostic down a sidestreet

Pulmonary submarine with soggy thud

A blot-out even of the larger stars

Glisten on specked eye leaking a long tear

Slickened condensation under park tree shadow

Disoriented unawake next morning

Somebody fumblingly seeks and seeks a lost addressbook

Smear-ringed moon and shriveled petals by the curb

Gurgling smells rise from the teeth of grates

Sharp heels clicking like a timer the Executrix

Yells recede leaving a clean moment

And I am set for liftoff these eyes filling with the sun

Static crackles as I clasp a few small words

A few live looks nod our complicity

For festal exposition of this waste

The Altered Moon

One giant step flattened the moon we knew,
cleft the lengthy stems of romantic dreams,
and began the end of that brief Lunar Era –
the few years when those bulky white-suited figures,
gold-visored, with their ghostly thick-booted bounds,
drawling in cheerful American through the chopped static,
trampled the grey virgin dust, scooped up some rocks,
and gazed momentarily at blue, cloud-marbled Earth
risen through void above the bleak airless horizon.

Nothing afterward, over a generation.

Then a different medium of imagination –
or means to its loss: from the "wasteland" of TV
fast-forward to flashy wireless web and podcasts'
indeterminacy. Disjunct. Omnipresent.

So now the curious craving to know more and more
about Earth's colourful, exotic neighbours – the orbs
with ice-rings, mega-storms, and cryovolcanoes –
is fed and served by robots through wide amplitudes
of spectral wavelengths, whose terabytes unveil
old glaciers under red dust of Mars, and black lakes
of ethane and weird dunes on smoggy Titan. – Worlds
far safer visited video-graphically,
with exponential anomalies to amaze
amateurs surfing the most alluring sites.

Mere spectacle for the specialist, never something
the entire world could watch together as one.

✧ ✧ ✧

Some of us once thought imaging Earth from the Moon
would leave her more precious to that collective One;
just as some hoped the demise of the Iron Curtain
would yield a great dividend, or the victory
of Capital could ease global agony.

Can anything like that, now, change peoples' minds;
or was it mere lunacy – the old wishing,
this asking for more than the one Man on the Moon?

Googling the Earth

Your paper maps were primarily reassuring:
their coastal curves, their colour-protocols.
The borders. Cage of longitudinal lines.

The disk that now blooms on your little screen, though –
flat patchwork globe, optical planisphere
which you can spin by the small white hand-icon
whimsically, until choosing to zoom on-in –

has, in its look, something vastly uncanny and monstrous.
The more so, if (slipped loose from any First World bias)
you make – say – Mother Africa swim to the fore,
her marvelously huge, tawny lobate contour,
surrounded by blue flaps of seas, filling your gaze's core.

There stretch Sahara, Nile, Rift, equatorial forests,
Niger and Congo. Namib. The Skeleton Coast.
The Atlas Range, far-opposite The Horn.
Gibraltar, polar-height from deep Cape of Good Hope.
Hemisphere-in-itself – or wide worlds galore.

✧ ✧ ✧

Don't yet plunge down anywhere there. Instead, just try this now:
the eeriest possible swerve that your nerved wrist can give.
Stop your tall orbit dead-calm on the central Pacific.
Engage its full-blue merely sprinkled with fly-speck atolls.

With all but thin-curved strips of continents forced to its rim,
this virtual emptiness glares darkly back up at you
as the unveiled Unconsciousness of a water-planet
utterly cleansed of amenities. Of solid ground.

But this too is Earth, though we've barely begun to know it.
Lidless, living Eye that vacantly gazes on-out,
as Jeffers wrote: never seeing the wakes of our wars.

View from My Balcony, October 11 '08

The doom of broken commerce cannot taint
the priceless mercy gilding this
illumination on the season's trees.

The sun need do no more than shoo
the traffic home with silent semaphore.

Let others reap the vacuum they have sown.

I know
where value is. Friends and the arts
of sound. The pulse
and ring and quiet swirl of coloured words.

May those who never lunged for riches wait
the panic out. Give local help. Expend
well-measured and immeasurable gifts.
– That substance which
they built up, stored, and keep regenerating.

Then is it not, also – far, far apart
from fraudulence, from aggravated cunning –
our primal course, our mission, *to bear through?*

Let the leaves fall.
                    The dead wood burn away.

We planted, and must hold, this other ground.

IV. The Vaster Stream

Six Acts of Flame

Some flame divides. There were those fiery swords
that pointed us from Eden. And the other
blowtorching fissures. The long brands of shame.

Most flame consumes. An intense flare, then soon
no remnant but loose ash torn by the wind.

Flame warms. It made us the more human once,
though now we can't put out the fires we lit.

Flame can refine: if what it's fed comes rife
with friable impurities whose loss
to smoke and floated slag enables ingots.

It will transform, when bloomed out of the mind
as an alchemic fusion-drive, ablaze,
that, squeezing the crass leaden lumps in things,

roars through their lax amalgam – to the gold.

Riddle

I am a lantern at noon, straining
to cast a midnight shadow that
will flicker a darkness not invisible
past any sunset, past any dawn.

I am a current in a long river
bent to deposit mineral traces
and crystal lattices in future stone.

I am a breath of an air aspiring
to birth snow-flurries onto an empty
desert valley, so new flowers blow.

I am the whirling millionth seed
intended to end as a permanent root –
and lantern-tree whose thick shape of shade
prints the ground above and below.

A Few Kinds of Blues

Fresh blue of distance.
Of the scattered sunlight,
vast, and safely transformed
… over domed air.

Blue surfaces, blue waves
that wrinkle and calm,
and mirror more deeply
the tint within
the clear ocean up-above.

And the earthly
edible blue of the only
blue foods I can think of –
blueberries and plums.
Oh – and blue cheese!

Then the blue of your eyes. That, most.
And pale blue of your veins.

So why, then, should blue stand
for sad?

In the Spirit of the Blues

after hearing Smokin' Joe Kubek and Bnois King
on the CD Chain Smokin' Texas Style

Blue-, white-, or no-collars, stiff collars, loose collars,
everyone who's nearly drowned in the blues
can still swim the music they gave their name to.

An ancient long river, blue-golden, that flows
through the veins of their form and sound. From scalps to toes,
we're inhabited by their dark sources and cause.

With them, misery's forestalled. Checked. Given pause.
Too true – they're engendered by sorrows and loss:
being poor, in love, lust, or by the drastic toss

of coin, deal of card, extra dip in the sauce.
Binge-drinking, pill popping, chain smoking; the hex
of the hard yearn for, absence of, excess of, sex.

Entrapments that shunt, betray, dispossess:

from which, nothing sounds out more deep, up the gut,
with as much howling energy, swagger, and strut,
what-ever the length of the mileage you log.

Whether strayed and rib-kicked like a lowdown stray dog
under lowdown mean-spirited crass cunning powers
or the craven, mean disrespect from someone humble;

however the snub or trip comes, and hard tumble,
when milk-and-honeyed hope embitters and sours,
The Blues is a life-lifter – yours and mine. Ours.

Variations After Piano

homage to Bill Evans (after someone said his sound was too pretty)

Thin brittle chimes, indigo-
tingling …
               Almost tentative, they half
configure, without ground, in eerie
        wistfulness, the first
   attenuated melody,   banish
banality from the obscure old standard,
        bend and steer
             its contours in
      and out of recognition,   weave
an icy starlight through the inmost ear …

Feeling, after-feeling, blown
   so finely cool, embodies thought
          that splays then into filaments
     whose active span goes no
more than a breath's:
        bereft
       of precedence, of link to thence or next;
   remote from the inchoate mist.

A last
    trickling caress
aligns as a swirled surge,   yet,
     for all the spangles of finesse
        along that tapered flourish,   this
   gestures, also, at
indefinacy:
             end   of its end, with
no sound,   without a place for,
   trace of, any
      habitation;   gone,   drawn on
      conclusionless

String Quintet

A limpid sorrow unveils its
pooled welling dark:
with implication
that the highest also suffer, while still those

left low, like us, may dwell acceptably
these moments in the gateless
garden of delicious sound,
whole and inspirited.

On Music

after Rilke, "An die Musik"

Music: the breath of statues.
Perhaps, the stillness in paintings.
You, speech where all speech ends.
You, time stood-upright on the heart's path.

Emotion –
and for whom? Metamorphosis
of emotion to *what?* A hearable landscape.
Strange locale, Music. Grown out
of our own heart-spaces. Out of the Inmost,
climbing us, to press beyond.

A sacred departure: when the Within
stands as remote
as the other side of the air.
Clean,
unbounded, and not
anyplace where we live.

Tu Fu's Pines

China, 8ᵗʰ Century (after a literal translation)

My four pines, when they were first transplanted,
stood just over half my height – and now,
after three years, they match me. Carefully,
I look them all over. … The roots hold strong.
the branches somewhat battered, but they
stretch their thin arms in shiny deepgreen.

I've escaped the rebels. I'm home. Spring grass
floods my yard, and my fence around the pines
is broken. Peace has not returned, so
I cannot claim this empty house, where
little is left. Much was ruined. Still,
to be back here is happiness. The caress
of a soft breeze brings a feeling of youth.

My pines – grow tall, and spread your shade.
I, a man without roots or ties, am your friend.
I sing poems. Consequences of these times
will soon drop away. And what use to speak
of my days to come? But you, pines, will rise
majestic into the skies.

Little Island

after the painting by A. J. Casson

This island grove rises like sculpted stone
in conic and sail shapes, white masts, and prow
full-dressed with mutated autumnal tones
above a stone-grey-sheening still lakewater
backed by cloud-masonry of solid powder.

A soft marmoreal monument to nature,
it spreads a quietude no wind will shake
through steady presence whose cool, slow intake
leaves perfect lonesomeness
                                         in the onlookers,
calmly arrested from the fluttered pulse
inside the mold of flesh; and *yours*, the maker's –
bonded yet separate. Gone away, and else,

resuming, out here, in there, not-quite-now,
then ever, between beats to nowhere   flown

Beloved Remoteness

after poems by Philippe Jaccottet

Star-fires shine on a black expanse
of indefinite separation.

Servants of telescopic thought
keep vigil through the hour before
the faint moon mists over.

Then, up higher than ear can soar,
re-poises the uneven balance
of summit and reverie,

until, full-across the actual ridge,
torrential light pours onto me.

All the while my inner coldness
is punished by this cold glare within
the smolder of time.

And yet the sun's resumption quickens
her persistent shadow, cast
down the canyon

and on, at the mirroring mouth.

Evanishments

an homage with borrowed phrases

The songbird that leapt beyond song
has gone, perhaps always.

Impassive dusk hears the cries
of absence and rubble.

Eyes half-empty of origin
widen for desperate names.

Sporadic sparks erupt
under light so dim.

What have we been, or what are we not,
apart from our wanting?

One may excel at mending rips
but the ink goes pale on the page.

A breath blown from nowhere, Joy
only visits a dream.

Do I subscribe to anything now
besides desire?

With a faint shimmer, night's gifts
dissolve in the dew.

Like headlands astern of a ship,
the magi of sleep recede.

Life / Hope

after Henri Michaux, "Mon Vie"

Nominal life, you go it
your own way. Trek

off ... And I'm
so tentative.

You scrap, you
skirmish in some other district

while the home flame
dies down.

This mis-
match duo never did catch on.

Where are
your trophies? The take?

You do not
deliver what would satisfy. So,

thanks to you
my aspirations fly

into the stratosphere

Condition

variation on "I rise with an effort" by Philippe Jaccottet

Painfully I get up and observe
three divisions of light: the high sky,
the one whose drench my body absorbs,
and that sending the shade from my hand.
(These inked lines could be taken for such.)

I did not expect the sky's downturn.

One might have wished that the effort made
to describe the first light justified
suffering. But pain itself outweighs
any endeavour to soar above.

A great pity floods this entire plain,
and the night's eyes are spangled with tears.

Two Good Angels

variations on poems by Rafael Alberti

1. Illuminant

A passageway in the chest
that admits ocean.

House whose portals lighten
the wide neighbourhoods.

Rooftop more firmly emplaced
than girder or marble.

An aria! across gusts
of puffed lindenbloom.

Every surface more mellow
for touches beneath

so open a palm. A baton
waves up fresher choirs.

The jovial, seraphic one
induces, persuades

access to that and this by
sheer generous tone.

Deep laughter. Fountain. Bright fort
of nourishing sound.

2. Waterer

Without being sought, the vital one,
the one most needed,
came near us.

Not the kind,
all forehead and straight-arm,
who blocks out the moon.

But one beyond projection.
Whose lyric imprint
is a light that breathes.

Whose bell-
clear listening, of itself,
calls eloquence from shy mouths.

Whose own talk is vintage;
rays from which reach
into softening bedrock.

Whose moisture draws greening thoughts
through crevices
and from the prime loam.

3. A Disclaimer

And I let the little lake name them,
this air inspirit a tenuous
cosmogony, and the clouds of May
mime substance. Also the sun

and mottled moon be stand-in, cipher
for two putative souls; and several
planets image the gravity
and scale of their wills.

They could never lodge in my city.
On earth: where humans only
mangle our flimsy scaffolds and
waste gifts.

What we dare argue becomes, at hottest,
fireworks that singe us.
Contrivances keep
sputtering from splits in our tongues.

✦ ✦ ✦

Still, sometimes, one singular person –
through what he chooses, *and is* – enacts,
despite the erosions around us,
angelic analogies.

Some Parts of the Journey

1.

Sweep the ashes away! Appletrees,
in bloom against open blue, are raising
warm illusory snow; the thunder
retreated. So may all our eyes
taste this one florescence
and sip nectar from
its weightless space, before
the whole pavilion shreds.

2.

The evening clouds return, not
unlike a longing: the goldenglow
superseded by carmine. How they
undress the done day. Dissolute,
yet yielding, past vision, a trust
that wants no foundation – a trust
in new beginning, light out of dark
beyond solar imaging.

3.

Incomprehensible impetus flung
the curtains apart. In faded light
we recognize contours. Furnishings.
Now through the window on dusk
the torch of Venus burns large.
Inducements to love
resound, here at the summit of summer.
So let us mingle our breaths.

4.

Those innocent gifts to each other
were partaken. Consumed in the flesh.
Barefoot on the given grass we strayed .
far, near, as we willed.
How could we have known how or when
the two of us had already turned
from the arena of darkening morning
and left ourselves in a dream?

5.

Why should we wish, then, to scrape
at the cinders of whatever
we had once been? We consign that
to the black flames from oncoming night –
and ally with close cold stone and its
inclusions of mica. Yet, maybe, also,
somewhere, somehow we still weld
by the sparks of the stars.

6.

Our shadows received earthen tints.
Unhurt, they bounded with us
over well-ignored rocks. Crevasses.
At times we were crossed
by other shadows – buzzards or hawks.
But the met press of our cheeks
loosened us from
the tethers that are earthen words.

7.

The borders on the old pathways
grew through to each other, and dry
stepping-stones have submerged.
This embrace becomes that of
a blocked light as much as of arms.
Still – entering age – winter night
unveils its own long luminescence.
Bare trees enlarge over snow

and over the moon's blanching
their foliage becomes air,
and the tips point in, out and up,
far past the most rarified curve.
At final dawn, any spaces we charted,
in transparence or opacity,
will no longer have measure. Their shade
will empty on everywhere.

Age

After the wild, windy nights on nights
away from the initial gate,
your passion and rages only dissolve
in the uniform rigor of morning:
the strain of the dark shaken off
as if among waking known birds.

Now fully set for the shrinkage
of new shadows, you leave step by step
whatever you were while still wanting
to wrench from time's ballast, and slide
into irises gracing an embankment,
or back to long-forbidden glades.

And yet, with your restless wound
and traveler's seasoned disinterest,
you bear on-ahead past the day, and past
the next pool of wider twilight, on
and on toward the estuary of all,
nearer what you felt you were seeking:

atop the terminal cliff that reveals
through agile grasses over cold spray
by the last cascade in definitive glimmer
the ridge of no more and of everything less,
where you lean, unable to be alarmed
as the greater forgetting begins –

in numb wilderment at the sea-fowl crossing
the beds of the moon and the sun.

Fluidity

Whether or not the flame
and lively air flee away, still there
is under-flow – even under
the fundament and the rock.

The current on whose course I go
will, when I strand, retain that flow
beyond my relics, the old and new jails,
the levees, the forts, the worn stones, their names.
And I'll have lent something. Ripple of heat?

Today I shift in the channel, again
allowing the outlines of florid dreams,
their ashen entrails and smoke, to diffuse
to oblivion.
                    How could I have wanted
their voices aloud, their shadows abroad,
have let the flamboyant ships blockade me,
when I know all such tinder of cloud
had best burn and drown.

The sun soon washes the latest half-mirror
clean. It's as though double death below
the beds below nightmare (of one's only end
and that of the earth) were wholly a lie.

But the passing foam astern, and the prow
of futurity, unsteered, unseeable,
and the in-between filament of the now
bewilder forever.

The very vessel I am, itself
enflamed, has noisy bulk enough
to hide heaven's memories, false and true,
in its twined intake of pleasure with pain.

The stricken moil emits the light
and shade of its own unsung dream.
And a truer one, now: the one that refutes
and refuses extinction. This transparence, this
firm waver and wake in which I thrive
and move, under cool of the stars –

to re-ignite, below-core, behind
mere sourcing or placement,
apart from all
that was anything other – on into what next
will assume this inveterate flame.

The Amicable Stars

variation on Jorge Guillén, "A la vista"

Amidst the sonorous night the stars
accompany our minutes and hours
inaudibly to the human ear.

With a shrewd brilliance they glitter and
resolve: configured, atremble, above
the many mysteries. Never unsure.

We're tormented by our understanding?
Those huge spaces will always leave us
shy before their outrageous immensity.

Space beyond space ... of withheld revelation
so far apart from our thought, that it calls:
Wait; don't give yourselves up to delirium.

The sky over our hearths is housing –
familiar, and well-named – these stars, who,
paradoxically, become friends.

Author's Notes

The poems in *Confluences* flow from multiple streams. Personal experiences, anxieties, and convictions are enlarged by my readings, especially of European poetry (mainly in translation), and merge with such other influxes as music, visual art, and even writing exercises. This plurality of sources and interests is most evident in the last section but permeates all four.

I. Antiquity – Forerunners of all but three of these poems were in the art and poetry book *Temple of Fire* (LyricalMyrical, 2008), one of whose main themes was the classical and pre-classical world – or what can be known and imagined of it. A half dozen poems here were fairly direct responses to my wife Holly's artwork. Although some research was done, the reflections on ancient times and ancient themes don't presume to be comprehensive or authoritative. I hope it will also be clear that the admiration expressed for the ancients is not entirely unreserved.

II. Impress of Waters mixes some of my newer "nature" poems together with much earlier ones, including four from another LyricalMyrical book, *Urban-Pastoral* (2004). All of these poems are set in different times and places, with the exception of the relatively recent "Green Music" and "Strata Before Sunset," which are from my balcony in Thornhill, as is the last poem in section III. "Dec. 31, '08" was written while house-sitting on Mill St. in Thornhill; and "Urban Pastoral with Crows" comes from a previous residence which overlooked Toronto's "Annex" neighbourhood.

III. Conditions – The poems here tend to be more abstract and opinionated. "Reflections on *Gojou*" came out of a writing exercise from Diane Mascherin, related to a Japanese notion of "the five passions." Having as many as five poems here on climate change reflects my belief that this all-too-familiar topic demands continued, and varied, treatments. "Atmosphere, October 2008" owes a debt to an untitled poem by Pëters Brüveris, translated from the Latvian by Inara Cedris in the anthology *The Baltic Quintet* (Wolsak & Wynn), p. 121. "On Twisted Streets" is indebted to the Kenneth Rexroth translation of Reverdy's poem.

The last line of "Googling the Earth" revisits the ending of Robinson Jeffers' "The Eye": "this is the staring unsleeping / Eye of the earth; and what it watches is not our wars."

IV. The Vaster Stream – All of the poems here came about through other means than direct experiences like the walks and travels of section II, or ideas and arguments such as those in III. "A Few Kinds of Blues" and "In the Spirit of the Blues" are from writing exercises and challenges, as is "Call" in the previous section. Several others, obviously, were responses to specific works of music and art. Among many Bill Evans recordings, I particularly had in mind his rendition of Paul Simon's "I Do It for Your Love" on the CD *The Paris Concert: Edition One*. "String Quintet" was originally part of a longer poem inspired by Mozart's K. 614. The painting *Little Island* is at The McMichael Collection in Kleinburg ON.

More than a dozen poems in this part of the book are homages and adaptations into English (not translations) written "after" a number of eminent poets' writings in other languages. They aim, not immodestly, for a certain equivalence, rather than to imitate or echo. Most of the source-poems and poets are credited in my italicized subtitles, but I wish to acknowledge these additional debts:

I consulted several translations of Rilke's "An die Musik," including Stephen Mitchell's.

"Tu Fu's Pines" is a version of "The Four Pines" as translated by Rewi Alley in *Du Fu Selected Poems,* published in China by Foreign Languages Press, ISBN 7-119-02889-8/1-695.

"Beloved Remoteness" and "Evanishments" were derived in part from phrases in several poems by Philippe Jaccottet and by Yves Bonnefoy, respectively: all of them in *The Vintage Book of Contemporary World Poetry,* ed. J.D. McClatchy. The respective translators are Derek Mahon and Lisa Sapinkopf.

Henri Michaux' poem was translated by Bernard Waldrop, among others.

The style, if not the mood, of "Two Good Angels" emulates poems in Rafael Alberti's *Concerning the Angels*, translated from the Spanish by Christopher Sawyer-Lauçanno. "Fluidity" also came out of my reading of that book.

Each stanza of "Some Parts of the Journey" is a response to one of Bonnefoy's "Stone" poems (all titled "Un Pierre"), translated by Hoyt Rogers in the bilingual book *The Curved Planks*.

"Age" is built from borrowed and altered phrases I found in the poem "Octet Before Winter" by Claire Malroux, translated from the French by Marilyn Hacker.

"The Amicable Stars" was a response to Jorge Guillén's poem, translated by Cola Franzen in the bilingual *Horses in the Air and Other Poems*.

I hope readers of the above poems will be intrigued enough to go on to explore the impressive bodies of work of those to whom I pay homage: "vaster streams" indeed. I believe that, even at a time of much global dread, among the many legitimate, confluent motivations for the poetry I most care about are the impulses of celebration and gratitude, the wish to pay tribute, and the insatiable desire to discover and learn.

Acknowledgements

Versions of most of the poems in this book appeared previously in the literary journals and zines *The Ambassador, Lichen, The Literary Review of Canada, p o e t r y z'o w n, Vallum,* and *Verse Afire;* in the anthologies *Arborealis, The Book of Thighs, Earth to the Moon, Feast of Equinox, Frost and Foliage, Gojou, Opus III: A Conspiracy in XV Variations, Poets for Life, Renaissance Reloaded, Sounding the Seconds,* and *Waging Change: Vaughan Poets Engage in Politics;* and in the limited-edition LyricalMyrical books *Galactic Music, Temple of Fire,* and *Urban-Pastoral.* I wish to thank the editors and publishers of those anthologies, including Mark Clement, Dina Ripsman Eylon, Richard Grove, Katherine L. Gordon, I.B. Iskov, Jim Lanthier, Diane Mascherin, and Debbie Ouellet, and to express my particular gratitude to LyricalMyrical publisher Luciano Iacobelli.

Further thanks go to Donna Langevin and the Artbar poetry group; to Diane and the gang in the Toronto Renaissance Conspiracy; to Dina and Debbie and the Vaughan Poets' Circle; to John Reibetanz and the Vic poets; to those, including James Dewar, Michael Fraser, and Marja Moens, who provided the "challenges" and exercises which resulted in some of these poems; and to all who have generously given me wise advice, moral support, and constructive criticism in my writing endeavours.

Al Moritz and John Reibetanz have my deep appreciation and gratitude for their invaluable help at two crucial stages in this book's progress.

I am also very grateful to Maureen Whyte for her belief in the book and commitment to it.

Most of all, thank you, Holly, for your many tributary confluences – and for everything.